Sparktacular Kids Presents

The Cupcake Kid: Mia's Entrepreneurial Journey

Publisher: Sparktacular Kids
Copyright @ 2023 Stephen Duffy
All rights Reserved

Chapter 1

Ravenhill Park was always busy on a Saturday, especially in the summer, and today was no different. Mia trailed behind her Mum as she walked a path that twisted around the park's edge.

Around Mia, dozens of people lazed in the sun. Mia could see a group of college students throwing a Frisbee on the open meadow while being chased by a very enthusiastic shaggy sheepdog.

A man with a wide-brimmed hat and floral shirt painted a picture of a bridge over a river. At least Mia thought it was supposed to be a bridge; it could have been a fish or a very oddly shaped potato. It was not a very good painting, but the man looked like he was enjoying himself.

A band was setting up on the bandstand, being watched by a man slathered in so much sunscreen Mia first thought he'd been attacked by a paintbrush.

People were generally having a great time, playing catch, reading books, and walking their dogs. Well, almost everyone was having a great time. Mia usually loved the park on a Saturday, but today her Mum had decided she was going to finally get fit, and that meant instead of their usual stroll through the park, her Mum was power walking aggressively, hips swaying dramatically from side to side as Mia hustled to keep up.

Mia's face was dripping with sweat, her hair was tied back in a tight ponytail, dark patches were collecting in the armpits of her new top, and her sunglasses kept threatening to fall off as they bounced on the edge of her nose.

Mia was so distracted looking longingly at the queue for the ice cream truck that she didn't hear the ringing of bells until they were right on top of her. Looking behind her, she saw three kids on bikes hurtling towards her.

Mia leapt off the path as the bikes whistled past. Mia stared in amazement, and the shining machines raced up the trail.

"Mum, Mum, did you see?" Mia called her mother.

"Mia, why are you lying on the grass? You will ruin your new clothes," Mum said, stopping and breathing hard.

"I think they are already ruined," Mia mumbled, looking at the dark sweat patches under her arms.

"What was that?" Mum said, eyebrow raised and foot tapping.

"Did you see?" Mia replied, hurriedly getting back to her feet and brushing some dirt off her jeans.

"See what, dear?" Mum replied.

"The bikes, Mum. How did you not see?" Mia continued to look up the path where the bikes had disappeared from sight. "They were amazing."

"Oh yes, they were very nice," Mum replied.

"Nice? They were amazing. I want one. Can I have one?" Mia looked at her Mum hopefully.

Mum looked at her, considering. "Sorry, dear, but those bikes are expensive."

Mia ducked as a football flew over her head. "Please, Mum, I need one." Mia could see herself flying through the park on her brand-new bike.

"Sorry, Mia, but we can't afford one of those bikes."

"Mum…"

"That's enough, Mia." Mum took off again up the path. "Come on, we can get another lap in before we have to head home."

Mia looked down at her stained and muddy clothes. "But mum." It was too late; her Mum was already out of earshot. Mia scrambled to catch back up, but she couldn't get the image of those shiny bikes out of her head.

Chapter 2

Mia sat moping at the kitchen table while her Mum made dinner. Mia pushed a salt shaker around the table, still dreaming of those bikes.

"How does kale and broccoli soup sound for dinner?" Mum asked.

"Truly awful," Mia replied, scrunching up her nose.

"Come on, Mia, it'll be good for you. Kale is a superfood, you know." With her new health kick, Mum had cleared out the kitchen of everything even remotely tasty.

Instead, the inside of the refrigerator looked more like a forest than a fridge.

"Pizza is a superfood," Mia replied.

"Mia, what have I said about.."

BANG - Mia jumped as the front door closed, announcing the arrival of Mia's Dad and saving Mia from a scolding.

"Hello," he shouted from the hall.

"In here," Mum replied.

Mia returned to pushing the salt shaker around, still moping.

"Hello, Mia." Mia ignored her dad continuing to huff at the table.

"What's wrong with you?"

"She's upset. She wants a new bike," Mum said while chopping up a particularly chunky piece of broccoli.

"A new bike!" Dad replied. "That's interesting. I had a bike when I was younger. I loved it."

"You see, Dad, that's why I need one," said Mia, suddenly excited.

"You don't need one, sweetie; you want one. There is a difference," Mum responded.

"But...."

"Your Mum is right, Mia. Bikes are expensive. If you want one, you will have to pay for it yourself," Dad said.

"How am I supposed to do that. I don't have a job," Mia protested.

"Guess you will have to figure that out."

"I guess I will," Mia replied. If no one would help her, then she would do it herself.

"What's for dinner?" Dad asked, pulling out a seat across from Mia.

"Kale and broccoli soup," Mum replied cheerily.

"You're joking!" Dad exclaimed, looking almost as green as the soup.

Chapter 3

Mia sat with her legs crossed on her bed, a copy of the local paper spread out in front of her. Dinner had been an unmitigated disaster. Mia could still hear her dad being sick in the bathroom.

Mum was calling through the bathroom door, "I just don't understand what happened."

"Maybe we should have less kale the next time," Dad replied before belching violently again.

"But it's a superfood." Mia wasn't sure her dad heard that over the sound of his vomit.

Mia tried to tune them out as she turned her attention to the paper's job section. Time to find a job. If no one would buy her a bike, she would have to do it herself. Her eyes scanned down the Job listing:

IT Support worker - Probably not, Mia thought; she had once tried to play a game online and accidentally downloaded a virus. Dad lost 3 weeks' worth of work and had been very annoyed.

Construction worker - Mia tried flexing her biceps a couple times but thought this one wasn't for her.

Lawyer – Mia could see herself shouting objection and questioning witnesses like those lawyers on TV, but you probably needed qualifications to do that.

Chef, Taxi driver, paramedic. The list went on and on. And Mia wasn't qualified for any of them.

"Why is this so hard?" Mia said to no one as she flicked to the final page of advertisements. Being eight years old probably didn't help with her job prospects. Mia had almost given up hope when she came to the last advertisement.

SHOP ASSISTANT WANTED.

"I could do that." Mia could see herself staking shelves, collecting money, and wishing customers a good day. And the shop was right down the street. Mia's Mum shopped there at least once a week. This was perfect.

Mr Baxter's shop was quiet this early on a Sunday morning.

BRIIINNNGG – a slight ringing sounded as Mia pushed open the heavy door. The store was small and cluttered with all manner of sweets, magazines, fruits, cleaning products, coffees and milk. Everything you could need.

The shop was always busy but could have been more organised if you asked Mia. Who would put the milk beside the soap and the cereals next to the toilet cleaner?

Mia had seen someone suggest reorganising the store to Mr Baxter once; he told them to get out and never come back. Mia had been scared of Mr Baxter ever since. But not today. Today she was going to put on a brave face. Mia needed a bike; to get that, she needed a job, and Mr Baxter had the only job available that Mia was suitable for.

Mr Baxter was behind the counter when Mia walked in. He was a tall man with a square head and a serious face. He loomed large over the counter like a giant or an ogre.

"Hello," Mia called when she arrived at the counter, which she could barely see over.

"What do you want?" Mr Baxter replied.

"I need a job," Mia said with a smile.

Mr. Baxter laughed. "Do you now? And why is that?"

"I want a new bike. Mum and Dad said I need to pay for it myself."

"Ah, I see." Mr Baxter replied with his deep voice. "And why exactly would I want you to work here?"

"I'm a hard worker. I can work the register and stack the shelves," Mia said, eager to impress. Mia could see herself on the bike already with a fistful of cash left over from being the best shop assistant in the world.

"No!" Mr. Baxter boomed. He didn't even take a second to think about it.

"What? Why?" Mia questioned as she saw her dreams crashing down around her.

"Too young, too small," Mr Baxter's deep voice filled the whole shop. A couple of older kids had come into the store while Mia had been talking. They were pointing and laughing at her now.

"BUT!" Mia protested.

"No but's, no job," Mr Baxter boomed. "You don't just get a job because you want one."

Mia was so angry and annoyed she didn't know what to say. Mr Baxter just stared at her with his big, serious head.

"Fine, I'll start my own shop then," Mia replied. Mia could hear Mr Baxter laughing as she stormed out of the shop.

Mia marched into her house, still bubbling with anger at Mr Baxter. Mum was in the kitchen, poking through a box of vegetables on the counter.

"What's got you all upset?" Mum asked.

"Mr Baxter said I'm not good enough to work for him!"

"I'm sure he didn't put it like that."

"He did!!!" Mia protested. "I'm going to prove him wrong."

"I'm sure you will," Mum replied, distractedly holding an overly large mushroom up to the light.

"Yeah, I don't need him. I'm going to start my own shop and make my own money. I don't need a job."

HAHAHA.

Mia turned to the sound of laughing. Her older brother Tom was laughing from the doorway.

Tom was three years older than Mia and was always making fun of Mia and her ideas.

"You don't know anything about running a shop," Tom continued laughing. "Kids can't just start shops. You're so stupid."

"Leave her alone, Tom," Mum said.

"I'll learn. I'll prove you all wrong." Mia did her best to ignore her brother, still laughing as he left the room.

"Sure you will, pipsqueak," Tom called back. "When you are done, maybe you could also solve world hunger or become a movie star."

"I'll show him," Mia whispered to herself.

Chapter 4

"Mum, I need to open a shop," Mia said.

Mia sat on the living room floor, drawing pictures of what she thought her new store would look like. It had floor-to-ceiling windows to let the light in. The shelves were overflowing with stock and much better organised than Mr Baxter's stupid store.

"I like the idea Mia, but you just can't open a shop." Mum explained, "You need products and a building before you get customers. All that takes money, a lot of money."

Mia sat down at the table, upset. She didn't know what to do next. She could see exactly what she wanted; a shiny, glistening new shop full of food, sweets and, most importantly, customers. Mia imagined how much money she would make with a shop like that. She would be able to buy her bike in no time.

But how would she start a shop like that? She had no money.

Mum gave her a hug. "You are on the right track; you just need to start smaller."

"Smaller?" Mia wondered, mind already spinning. "I can do that."

The next day, Mia was moping around the playground at school. She could see her friends having fun: Christie was rocking on the swing, and Dylan showed Dan some moves on his skateboard. She could see Fred in the library through the window, hunched over his computer, no doubt working on the next edition of the school paper.

Mia couldn't enjoy any of it, still dreaming about a new bike and trying to figure out how to start her shop. She was sitting on a bench in the corner of the playground, knees drawn up to her chest, twisting a shoelace through her fingers when she heard someone calling her name.

"Hey Mia," Sophie called, running in Mia's direction.

"We are about to start a game of netball. Wanna play?" Sophie and Mia had been best friends for as long as Mia could remember. Sophie's long hair blew about her face as she dropped onto the bench beside Mia.

"Maybe later," Mia responded.

"What's wrong?" Sophie asked.

"Nothing, I am just thinking." Mia continued to mope.

"Really, it's not like you to mope about. You love netball. Come on, tell me; maybe I can help."

Mia looked around to make sure no one was listening. Mia shuffled closer to Sophie, "I'm going to open my own shop."

"Really!" Sophie squealed, "Where? What are you going to sell? When are you going to open?"

Mia sunk lower on the bench, looking stressed. "What's wrong?" Sophie asked.

"I am going to open a shop. I just can't think of where to start. I don't know where

I'm going to open or what I'm going to sell. I don't have any money."

"Maybe I can help. Why don't you come over to my house tonight, and we can come up with ideas?" Sophie offered.

Mia smiled happily, "That's a great idea!"

"Fantastic," Sophie said. "Now, let's go play some netball, and we will make a plan later."

Mia felt better and ran after Sophie laughing.

Chapter 5

Sophie's room was a colourful mess. The walls were covered with posters of Sophie's favourite singer Dana as well as dozens of Sophie's own drawings. The girls sat on an aqua-blue carpet in the centre of the room.

"Where do we start?" Sophie asked.

"Let's come up with some ideas first. I need to know what I could sell," Mia said.

Sophie pulled out a notepad, and the girls started to make a list.

"Books?" Sophie asked.

"I love my books. I wouldn't want to sell them."

"Shoes?"

"Then what would I wear?"

"You could buy more." Sophie started. "Never mind, that doesn't make any sense."

Soon the list in front of Sophie was covered in ideas, none of which would work.

"Hi, girls. How's it going?" Sophie's Mum called as the door swung open, carrying a tray of lemonade.

"Not great. We still haven't got any ideas," Mia replied.

"Don't worry, I'm sure you will get there eventually. These things take time, patience and hard work," Sophie's Mum always saw the bright side of things. "It's hot in here. I thought you would appreciate some lemonade while you work."

"Thanks," Mia said as she reached for a glass.

"Yeah, thanks, mom."

Both girls drained their glasses quickly, suddenly realising how hot it was.

"Whoa, this is so good," Sophie said as she finished her lemonade.

"Yeah, this is great," Mia replied. The lemonade was fresh and left a slight tingle at the back of her throat. Coming up with business ideas was hard work.

Mia suddenly jumped up, scattering paper all over the floor. "That's it!"

"What?" Sophie looked on, confused.

"Lemonade!" Mia could barely contain her excitement.

"Yeah, that was lemonade. Are you alright?" Sophie asked, looking concerned.

"I'll sell lemonade. People run and walk by my house all the time. I can sell lemonade to them," Mia said, mind already running away with the idea.

"That's a great idea!"

Soon both girls were jumping around Sophie's room.

Chapter 6

Mia's parents were watching their favourite show, a singing competition called Music Idol when Mia burst into the living room. "I have an idea." Mia was hopping up and done in front of her parents, bursting with excitement.

"Mia, calm down. What are you talking about?" Dad said, shuffling in his seat to keep one eye on the TV.

"I'm going to start a lemonade stand," Mia said excitedly.

"Really, where did this idea come from?" Mum questioned.

"People are always running past our house, and it's so hot outside. They will all stop to buy my lemonade." Mia couldn't keep the smile off her face as her parents considered her plan.

"That's actually an excellent idea, Mia. What do you think?" Mum asked her dad.

"I think she is on to a winner," Dad said, although Mia wasn't sure if he was talking about her plan or Bella Del Martin, Dad's favourite contestant who had just finished a performance.

Mia clapped in excitement; she was going to take the win. "Come on, we need to go to the store. I need to get supplies. You said to start smaller. This is smaller. Please, Mum?"

"Ok, you have a good idea." Dad replied.

"Great, let's go to the store now," Mia demanded.

"After Mia, we need to wait until Idol is over. Now come sit down. The next act is about to start," Dad said, patting the seat beside him.

Chapter 7

The following day, the sun was high, and it was starting to heat up as Mia prepared her lemonade stand.

Dad helped her slide up the rusty garage door. The garage was a dusty mess, filled with years of discarded knickknacks and old furniture. An old bookshelf with a broken leg lay propped up against the back wall. Mia could see a couple of Tom's old sports trophies spilling out of boxes in the corner. Her old toy oven sat upside down, the door broken and hanging off.

"Dad, look at this! I used to love this oven," Mia said, trying to reattach the door.

"You sure did," Dad said, scratching his head, looking around at the garage. The dust floating up from the old boxes looked particularly thick in the sunlight. "Someone should really clean up in here," Dad said, poking a damp-looking box with his toe.

"Mum has been telling you that for years," Mia said, giving up on her old oven; it was beyond repair.

"Best not tell her I said that then," Dad said, hurrying away as if one of the old cupboards would jump up and bite him. "Good luck Mia," he called over his shoulder.

Mia spent a long time trying to set up a rickety old collapsible table in the middle of the garage. She had to slide a book under one leg to level it up.

She dragged two heavy coolers up beside the table and filled them both to the brim with bottles of lemonade. On top of the table, she set rows and rows of disposable cups for her future customers. It was tough work, and Mia was sweating by the time she was finished.

Her final touch was to hang a fancy sign she had designed, with Sophie's help, on the front of the table:

FRESH LEMONADE FOR SALE

Mia's heart was pounding with anticipation. Mia spotted the first pair of walkers from her perch behind the table as soon as they turned onto her street. Two women in workout gear sped down her street, running side by side. Great, Mia thought, they must be thirsty.

Mia got more and more excited as they drew closer. She could hear them chatting as they reached the end of Mia's driveway. Mia could barely take the excitement, and then it all fell flat as they kept walking without even looking in the direction of Mia's lemonade stand.

"Never mind, I'll get the next one," Mia said to herself.

The next person came running around the corner, moving quickly and listening to music. And again, they just kept running past Mia and her lemonade, without even looking in Mia's direction.

Mia could see her elderly neighbour Mr Winter leaving his house across the street. Mr Winter was a nice man, always smiling and asking Mia about school.

Mia watched as Mr Winter shuffled to the end of his driveway, his thin white hair poking up in every direction. His small circular glasses always perched on the very edge of his nose.

Mr Winter looked across at Mia. Mia got excited again; this was it, her first customer. Again, she was disappointed when Mr Winter made a confused face and turned in the opposite direction.

Mia stood by her table all morning. The same thing happened on repeat -people ran past all day, and not one person stopped. Mia abandoned her lemonade stand and went back inside, disappointed and upset. She dropped herself into a chair at her kitchen table.

"What's wrong, Mia?" Mum asked.

"No one stopped to buy any lemonade," Mia said.

"Really? No one! That's strange; on such a hot day, I would have thought you would have loads of customers."

"Me too. Dozens of people walked up and down the street, and no one came near my lemonade stand. I put so much work into setting up, and it was a complete waste of time." Mia responded.

"Don't give up so easily. You have a good idea. You need to work out the problem and fix it," Mum said.

Mia started to slide a salt shaker across the table. "I don't know what to fix, though. My shop is all setup and looks great in the garage."

"The garage? That's a long way from the street. Are you sure people knew you were selling your lemonade?" Mum asked. "The garage is a mess. Did your dad clean it?"

"Umm, no," Mia replied, not wanting to get dad in trouble.

"How many times have I told him to clean that garage?"

"Mum, we are talking about my lemonade stand," Mia interrupted before her Mum could start a rant and before Dad got in more trouble.

"Well, if your dad didn't clean it, then the garage is an absolute mess and very far away from the street. I bet no one even knows you are selling lemonade. And I know no one wants to go near that stinking garage."

"What do you mean? I have a great sign that Sophie helped me make," Mia questioned.

"People can't buy anything if they don't know you are selling. If no one was looking at the garage, they wouldn't see you, your sign or your lemonade."

Mia thought about what her Mum had said and realised her Mum was right. Mia had a problem but felt much better now that she knew what it was. Mia leapt up to make changes. "Thanks, Mum."

"No problem, and tell your dad I'm looking for him," Mum called after her.

Chapter 8

With Dad's help, Mia heaved her table and coolers to the edge of the garden. Soon she was set up right next to the street. It was another scorcher of a day, and Mia wore a wide-brimmed hat and oversized sunglasses.

Mia wasn't going to make the same mistake again. She knew the importance of advertising her products now. Mia spent the night before painting two more big signs to go with the one on the table.

Mia was delighted with her new setup. No one would miss her shop this time.

Behind her in the garage, her dad was sweating profusely, trying to move a mountain of old boxes. Guess Mum had a talk with him about the garage, Mia thought.

Mia grew excited as she heard the sound of the first runners approaching.

The two runners slowed as they saw Mia's refreshing lemonade.

"What's this?" asked one of the runners.

"Fresh lemonade. Just what you need when running on such a hot day," Mia said happily.

"Looks good to me. I'll take some," said the first runner.

"Me too," said the second.

The two gulped down two large glasses of Mia's lemonade.

"That was great!" one said, "We will stop again on the way back."

As the runners ran off, Mia was beaming from ear to ear.

All day runners stopped, walkers stopped, neighbours stopped, and dog walkers stopped. They all stopped, and eventually, Mia ran out of lemonade.

After a long day selling her lemonade, Mia sat exhausted at the kitchen table. All the money she had earned was spread out in front of her on the kitchen table.

Mia was delighted. She stacked the notes on one end of the table and then piled the coins into little towers. Looking at all the money, it would not be long until she could afford her bike. Once she had it, she would ride straight past grumpy Mr Baxter.

Mia was counting her money when her Mum came into the room. "Mia, this is very impressive for one day's work."

"Thanks, Mum. I'll be able to get that bike very soon."

"It might take a little longer than you think, Mia."

"What do you mean?" Mia asked confused

"Well, you can't just keep all this money. You have to pay for your supplies. The cups, signs, and the lemonade all cost money," Mum explained.

"But, but.." Mia babbled as she watched her Mum start to slide money back across the table and into her pocket.

"Plus, you will have to pay for more lemonade if you want to have any to sell tomorrow," Mum continued, sliding more money across the table.

"But that'll mean I lose most of my money," Mia protested.

"That's how business works, Mia," Mum explained. "You have to put money in to get money out."

"But it'll take me ages to make enough money like this." Mia put her hands on her head. "How do shops make any money?"

"Well, they sell lots of different things. Some things make them more money than others," Mum said patiently.

Mia thought about what her Mum had said. She needed to make more money to pay for all her product and still make enough money to save for her bike.

Mia came up with a new plan. She decided she would have to increase the price of her lemonade.

Chapter 9

The next day Mia set up her table just like before. The sun was high in the sky, and the day was heating up. In short, it was a perfect day for selling lemonade.

The only difference was today, Mia had increased her prices.

Mia was nervous. She could feel butterflies fluttering around in her stomach. What if her customers were mad? What if they shouted at her? What if they didn't buy any lemonade? What if yesterday was all just luck?

Initially, it was slow, but before long, Mia had a queue of people waiting on lemonade. A few people asked about the increased price, but most didn't. Before long, the money was rolling in.

By the end of the day, Mia had sold more lemonade than ever before, and with the increased price, Mia had made plenty of profit.

Mia was stacking her money on the kitchen table when her mom entered.

"Wow, Mia, looks like you had an even busier day today!" Mum exclaimed.

"Yeah, it was great. I sold all of my lemonade again. I think increasing the price was a great idea," Mia said.

"Looks like it was," Mum replied.

The following day was roasting hot, and Mia had even more lemonade prepared to sell. Mia stood behind her table, rows of cups lined up neatly. Signs positioned perfectly. The only problem was she didn't have any customers.

Mia didn't know what the problem was; the morning was quiet. Really quiet; no one came near Mia or her lemonade.

Late in the morning, a few people walked past. "Can I interest you in some lemonade?" Mia called out as the strangers walked by, hoping she would get some sales today.

"No, thanks, we have already had some!" they called back. Mia thought that was strange, but she figured they must have had some lemonade at home.

The day was scorching, and Mia was sweating under her wide-brimmed hat. She was also very frustrated – where were her customers?

Mia didn't know what to think. No one was interested in her lemonade. It was halfway through the day, and she hadn't sold any!!!

Mia spotted another group coming down the street. This was it; she was going to get some sales today. As they got closer, Mia spotted they were all carrying cups filled with lemonade. Mia was horrified; people must be getting their lemonade from somewhere else. She set off to investigate.

Mia stormed up the street. As soon as she turned the corner, she saw her problem. Mr Baxter's shop was at the top of the road, and signs advertising fresh lemonade were all around it. Even worse, Mr Baxter was selling the lemonade for half the price of Mia's.

Mia was so angry she stormed into the shop, past all the waiting customers and went straight up to the counter where Mr Baxter was smiling. His big square head loomed over Mia.

"You stole my idea!" Mia said, upset.

"I don't know what you mean," said Mr Baxter sternly, raising his bushy eyebrows.

"The lemonade, you stole my idea. I was doing it first," Mia said, even angrier.

"It's not about who does it first. It's about who does it better. And I bet you can't match my prices," Mr Baxter smiled menacingly.

"That's not fair!" Mia protested, knowing that she couldn't match his prices.

"Competition isn't supposed to be fair. It was a good idea though I have loads of customers. Now, if you don't mind, I have customers to serve," Mr Baxter said as she turned away.

Mia didn't know what to do; she stormed away and could hear Mr Baxter laughing at her. This was the second time Mia had left Mr Baxter's store upset, the sound of his laughter following her out the door.

Mr Baxter had beaten her this time, but Mia decided she wouldn't give up.

She had a new problem; she just needed to figure out how she would solve it. Mia knew she could do it now. She could solve problems. She could be successful. She would show Mr Baxter.

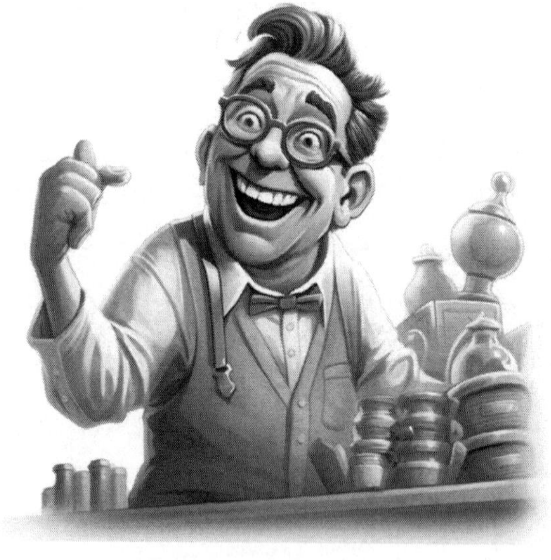

Chapter 10

Mia would not give up now that her lemonade stand had been a success; she just had to think of a way to make it more successful.

Mia paced around her room which was neat and organised as always. Her bed was up against one wall, an old movie poster hung above it on the wall, and a desk sat beside the open window. Mia's drawings of her ideal shop were stacked on the desk, her coloured pencils lined up perfectly beside the pictures.

Mia could hear the sounds of her friends playing outside, drifting in through the window. Mia ignored the noise; she had a problem to solve. At the moment, it seemed like an impossible problem. Mia needed to sell more lemonade to make a profit but to sell more lemonade, she would need to lower prices to compete with Mr Baxter. But if she lowered prices, she wouldn't make any profit. No profit meant no bike.

Mia went around this problem in her head before flopping down onto the bed.

"Uhhh, why is this so hard," Mia said to no one. "No, I can do this," Mia answered herself.

The pictures of her ideal shop, stacked on the desk, drew her attention. Shelves filled from floor to ceiling, stacked full of food and drinks. An image of her dream shop appeared in her mind, bright and shining.

The realisation hit her like a train. A thunderbolt of genius.

She needed to expand and add something new, something unique, something Mr Baxter couldn't just copy. It needed to be something that she could sell for more profit.

Ideas tumbled through her mind. But they were all too big or too small.

Mia was pacing again. The key, Mia thought, was that word unique. Her new product couldn't be something like lemonade. If Mia could go to a shop and buy lemonade to resell, then Mr Baxter could do the same, except he could do it at a much larger scale and charge much lower prices.

"If I can't just buy it, then I need to make it," Mia said to the teddy bear perched on her pillow, watching her pace.

Suddenly, it hit her – a memory of a bake sale at school. A year ago, the school was raising money to repair the gym roof. Mia and her Mum baked cupcakes; two tables full of cupcakes. Everyone loved them. In fact, Mia and her Mum had raised the most money. Now the gym roof was fixed and not even a little bit leaky. If cupcake sales could buy a new roof, they could definitely buy a bike.

The more Mia thought about it, the more she thought it was a good idea. Cupcakes would be homemade, and she would have to make them unique so Mr Baxter couldn't just copy them.

The only problem was that Mia's Mum had done most of the baking the last time, and Mia wasn't sure of all the steps. Guess I better learn, Mia thought.

Mia burst out of her room and ran down the stairs shouting, "Mom, I need your help."

"What's up, Mia?" Mum asked, "How's the lemonade stand going?" Mum was throwing thick lumps of carrots into a large pot on the stove.

"Terrible! Mr Baxter stole my idea, and now I have no customers."

"What?" Mum exclaimed. She looked annoyed at Mr Baxter too. "That doesn't sound Like Mr Baxter; he always seems so friendly."

"Yeah, he's a real peach," Mia mumbled before continuing. "It's ok, though. I have a plan; I just need your help. I need you to teach me how to make cupcakes," Mia said.

"Cupcakes! Are you sure you wouldn't rather learn to make my new carrot and cabbage pie recipe?" Mum looked hopeful.

"Absolutely not," Mia answered, perhaps a little too quickly.

Mia perched on a stool, notebook in one hand, freshly sharpened pencil in the other, taking notes as Mum laid out the ingredients on the counter. Eggs, butter, sugar, flour and colouring.

"Are you paying attention?" Mum asked.

Mia was leaning over; she couldn't have been paying any more attention, "Yes. What's first?"

Mia watched closely as Mum made the first batch. Scribbling notes furiously. Her Mum was a master at work. Mixing and whisking, precise and efficient. Before long, Mia was peeking through the oven window as rows of perfectly formed cupcakes were rising in the heat.

"What do we do now?" Mia asked

"We wait. Then we let them cool; then we do the fun bit, the icing."

"Did someone say icing?" Dad popped his head through the kitchen door.

"For Mia, not for you. But if you are hungry, I can get you some cabbage and carrot pie?" Mum replied.

"Um, no, no, I don't want to bother you. You look hard at work," Dad started looking like he was having flashbacks to the kale soup.

"You know what? I'm not even hungry," Dad said, sweating just a little. "What? Coming now," Dad shouted over his shoulder, "I think Tom is calling me. I must go. Good luck with the baking." Dad's head disappeared before Mum could reply.

"Strange, I thought Tom was at his friend's house," Mum said.

"Anyway, can we go over these steps again?" Mia said, waving her notebook, wanting to avoid more distractions.

For the next week, Mia and her Mum made cupcakes every day. Mia learned everything she could from her Mum. With each new batch, she helped a little bit more. First, Mia helped with the mixing, then the whisking, and then the icing. At night after baking, she watched loads of baking videos on YouTube to get new ideas and tricks. Mia was always thinking about baking; her dreams were full of dancing cupcakes.

After a week, Mia was ready to try a batch by herself. Mia did everything just like her Mum had shown her. She measured the perfect amounts of flour, eggs, sugar and butter. Mia had never concentrated as much in her life. Finally, she slid the mixture into the oven. Her face and clothes were covered in flour. In fact, the entire kitchen was covered in flour and sugar. Somehow Mum managed not to make any mess. Mia was going to need to clean this up before Mum spotted it.

Mia paced back and forth, waiting for the mixture to bake. She was so excited; the first batch of her cupcake empire was almost ready. The timer was ticking away on the counter. Tik Tok, Tik, Tok. Time just stretched on and on.

BRING, BRING, BRING. The alarm sounded. Cupcakes ready.

Mia pulled on thick oven gloves. "Mum, they are ready," Mia called. A wave of hot air hit her in the face as she pulled open the oven door.

In front of her were two neat rows of cupcakes in a tray. And every one of them was a mess. All of her cupcakes were burnt and flat. They looked terrible and tasted worse.

Mia had tried to make everything perfect, and….. it was a complete disaster.

The whole thing was inedible, hard and burnt.

"Mum," Mia called again; she could feel her eyes watering. "Mum."

"Mia, what's the matter?"

Mia couldn't talk; she just held out her cupcakes' pathetic, burnt remains.

"Oh, Mia," Mum gave her a hug.

"I can't do it. I tried so hard, and my cupcakes are a mess. No one could eat these, never mind sell them."

"Things don't always go perfectly the first time. In fact, they almost never go right the first time or the second. But if it was easy, everyone would do it. So, the only question is do you want this?" Mum asked. She was sitting on the floor beside Mia.

"Yes," Mia mumbled, tears still running down her face. "I do. But."

"No buts," Mum was firm, "You get up, and you try again and again until you get it right."

Mum was right. Mia wiped her tears on her sleeve. "You're right. I need to try again."

The first attempt had been a disaster, but Mia wouldn't be beaten. She cleaned up. Dusted herself off and tried again and again and again. Each time Mia learned from her mistakes. By the end, Mia wasn't even sure how many attempts she had made. The kitchen was a mess; mountains of half-baked, over-baked, or misshapen cupcakes were piled up in shaky towers. Flour, sugar and sticky icing were everywhere. It would take hours for Mia to clean all of this up. Mia was exhausted and dirty. She was covered in flour and sugar and was pretty sure some of it was even in her ears.

But in front of her was a row of perfectly shaped, perfectly baked, perfectly iced cupcakes.

Mia was so happy she could cry. All the work, all the effort had been worth it.

"These are so good," Mum said.

"So good," Dad agreed. At least that's what Mia thought he said; his mouth was full of cupcakes.

Her Mum was really proud of her, and Mia was proud of herself.

Chapter 11

It was a new day when Mia dragged her table across the front yard again, setting up her cups and coolers on her front lawn. This time alongside her cups of lemonade, Mia had plates piled high with cupcakes. Cupcakes of all types, chocolate chip, blueberry, strawberry. They looked delicious if Mia did say so herself. And judging from the fact she kept catching her dad trying to steal some, she was pretty sure he agreed.

Mia was excited, really excited. And also, really nervous. Her stomach was doing backflips in her belly.

The first customers were a group of walkers making their way briskly down the street.

"Interested in some lemonade?" Mia asked

"No, thanks, we already had some at the shop," They answered together.

"Well, can I interest you in some cupcakes then? They don't sell cupcakes like this in the shop." Mia said, crossing her fingers and hoping they would say yes.

"Oh yes, these cupcakes look delicious. Did you make them yourself?" One of the walkers asked, licking her lips just a little.

"Sure did!" Mia smiled.

"Why not?" the first walker answered, lifting one of the blueberry cupcakes; her friend quickly followed.

MMMM – they gobbled down the delicious cupcakes right in front of Mia.

"Thank you, these are so good," the walkers said as they ran off. "We will tell all our friends about your great cupcakes."

Word spread about Mia cupcakes. More customers arrived, just a few at first, then a few more, then a lot more and soon there was a queue down the street. All her neighbours and friends were waiting to try Mia's cupcakes. And most of them were also buying lemonade to have with their cupcakes. Mia quickly ran out of cupcakes; her tables were empty except for a handful of crumbs and empty cups. Mia was back in business.

Mia's best friend Sophie arrived just as Mia was packing up. "Hey, Mia," Sophie shouted as she approached.

"Hey." Mia waved back.

"How's the lemonade stand going?" Sophie questioned as Mia continued to pack.

"Great! I've sold so much lemonade, but lemonade is old news. Cupcakes are my new thing."

"I love cupcakes. Have you got any left?" Sophie asked hopefully.

"Nope, sold out. Just crumbs left. But there is always tomorrow," Mia responded.

Sophie noticed the stack of money Mia had earned. It was piled up in a tin can on the corner, bulging with notes, and rattled with coins when Mia lifted it. "Whoa, did you make all that money today?"

"Yeah." Mia smiled proudly.

"That's so cool." Sophie was impressed. "Do you want to go to the park to celebrate?"

Mia thought about it before shaking her head. "I can't. I have to start making cupcakes for tomorrow."

Sophie was proud of her friend. "Good luck, can't wait to see the new bike," Sophie shouted as she left.

Chapter 12

After an even busier day, Mia sat counting her money. This time she separated the money into two piles. One pile covered the money she spent on supplies; the second was her profit.

"Better day today, Mia?" Mum asked.

"Definitely! I think I'm getting the hang of this," Mia replied, "I would have made more if I hadn't run out of cupcakes."

"That's great dear. I heard people talking about your cupcakes at the hair salon," Mum said while fussing around the kitchen.

"Really?" Mia squealed excitedly. "What did they say? Tell me everything."

"Oh yes, you were the talk of the salon. Miss Rossbottom, you know her, she works at the bank. Her son used to go to your school. Oh, what was his name, Mark? No, Mike? Or maybe it was Jeremy."

"Mum! Never mind all that. What did they say about the cupcakes?" Mia interrupted her Mum, knowing that if she didn't stop her, Mum would never stop talking, and Mia would never hear about the cupcakes.

"What? Oh yes, the cupcakes. Well, Miss Rossbottom said they were amazing. So did Miss Chatterjee. But Miss Thompson and Miss Diamond were disappointed; you had run out by the time they arrived. Miss

Thompson said her husband was moping about the house because they missed out."

"That's terrible," Mia said, flopping back into her seat.

"No, it's great. I said they loved them." Mum looked at Mia, confused.

"Yeah, that's good, but other people were disappointed. You never want unhappy customers. That's bad for business." Mia could see Miss Thompson and her husbands' sad faces, crying into their dinner of kale soup, wishing they had some of Mia's cupcakes for dessert.

"Look at you, sounding like a proper businesswoman," Mum said.

Mia thought about her new problem. People loved her cupcakes, which was great. But she needed more; otherwise, people would be disappointed.

"I guess I need more!" Mia jumped out of her seat.

"More what?"

"Mum, preheat the oven," Mia said, wrapping her apron around her waist. "It's time to bake.

Mia immediately started measuring and mixing. Whisking and icing. Mum flew around her like a bee, following Mia's instruction. Mia spent the whole evening baking. She baked cupcakes in every flavour she could think of. Mia was exhausted when she crawled into bed with her cupcakes safely cooling in the kitchen

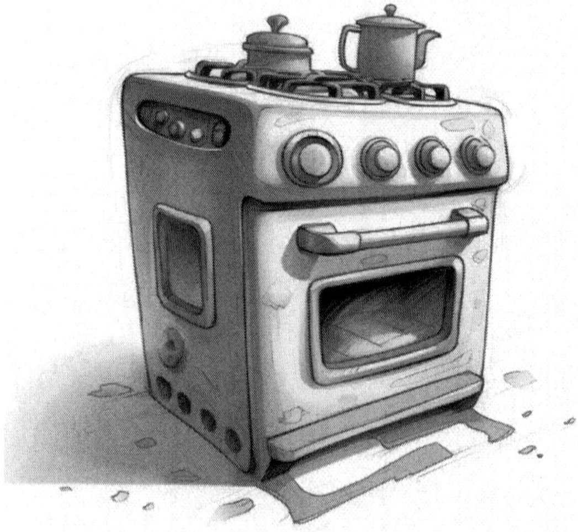

Chapter 13

The next day, Mia set up her table. The sky was a little grey, but the sun was just starting to peak through some gaps in the clouds. Mia had swapped her sunglasses and hat for a thick jumper and a hair band to keep blowing strands of hair out of her face. She set up her new sign, which read:

DELICIOUS CUPCAKES

Mia's table was piled high with different cupcakes —lemon, chocolate, vanilla, strawberry, and a dozen more.

People were already waiting by the time Mia finished setting up.

The day's first customer was Mrs Brown, an elderly lady with thick glasses and wispy hair. Mrs Brown bought three of Mia's chocolate cupcakes. "My grandson says these are the best cupcakes he's ever had," Mrs Brown said as she left.

The day grew busier and busier. The line down the street grew longer and longer. Just like the day before, Mia ran out of cupcakes.

The crowd groaned in disappointment when they realised the cupcakes were all gone. Mia was pretty sure she could see a couple of kids crying at the end of the queue.

"I'm sorry, everyone. There will be more cupcakes tomorrow," Mia told the crowd. All she heard back was more groaning.

Mia was packing her supplies when Mr Winter made his way slowly across the street. Winter was a good name for him, Mia thought; his skin was so pale, he was almost blue like the sky on a winter morning, his thin hair was sheet white, blowing in the breeze, and his circular glasses were perched on the tip of his nose, the glasses bounced around a little as he shuffled across the street.

He reminded Mia of an old, thin Santa Claus with glasses. Well, maybe he wasn't that much like Santa Claus, but he was definitely old and sometimes jolly.

"Hello, Mr Winter," Mia called happily, waving at him.

"Hello, Mia. I've heard so many good things about your cupcakes that I thought I would come over here and try one for myself," Mr Winter said. He smiled a crooked smile with more than a few missing teeth.

"Oh, I'm sorry, Mr Winter, but I have run out of cupcakes today," Mia apologised awkwardly.

Mr Winter sighed disappointedly, "Oh, that's alright. I guess I might try tomorrow."

Mia watched as Mr Winter made his way back home slowly. Mia hated having to turn customers away because she ran out of cupcakes. "Mum!" Mia called.

"Yes, dear." Mum's head appeared over the fence. She was wearing a green lycra suit, her head was wrapped in a yellow sweatband, and she was doing jazzercise in the backyard.

"Preheat the oven," Mia said, "Time to bake."

The following day Sophie helped Mia set up the table at the edge of the yard. As Sophie hung the For Sale sign, Mia lifted a box of freshly baked cupcakes and walked to Mr Winters' house.

Knock Knock

Mia waited a while before Mr Winter eventually opened the door. "Mia, what are you doing here?"

"I'm sorry I ran out of cupcakes yesterday, so I thought I'd deliver you some to make up for letting you down yesterday."

"Mia, that's very kind of you. Thank you. I'll be sure to tell all my friends how well you look after your customers."

Mia was delighted as she returned to finish setting up the shop. Mia knew that keeping her customers happy was the key to success.

Chapter 14

Mia sat on the living room floor, the TV was playing in the background, but Mia wasn't paying any attention. Mia was counting out the money she needed to buy baking materials before being interrupted.

"Where did you get all that money?" Her brother Tom questioned from the doorway. He was bouncing a basketball against the floor.

"Where do you think?" Mia replied, upset because she had lost count and would need to start again. "Be careful with that ball."

"No way your stupid lemonade stand is making that much money." Tom stepped closer, the basketball continuing to bounce at his side.

"Well, it is. Besides, it's not a lemonade stand anymore, and it's not stupid."

Mia could see Tom eyeing up her profits when she came up with an idea.

"You know I'd be happy to share some of this with you," Mia suggested.

Tom looked at Mia suspiciously, "Really? Why? What would I have to do?"

"I keep running out of cupcakes. That means I need to make more during the day, but I can't do that and sell at the same time," Mia explained.

"So, you want me to stand at your table and sell cupcakes while you bake more."

"Exactly!" Mia said.

"No way I'm going to work for you. Are you joking?" Tom said, getting angry. "I can get my own money."

"Then go do that then," Mia snapped back.

"I will." With that, Tom slapped his basketball at Mia, scattering her little towers of coins all over the floor. Coins rolled in every direction, and notes fluttered into the air. Tom's quick reactions snatched a few before he turned away.

"MOM!" Mia screamed. Tom was already disappearing through the door, ball in one hand, the other hand clutching some of Mia's hard-earned money.

Mia could hear him laughing as she scrambled to collect her scattered profit.

Chapter 15

"How have things been going?" Sophie asked. Mia and Sophie were making the short walk from the bus stop to Mia's house.

School had been busy. Mr Frost had been grumpy all day. He had set a mountain of homework. Mia wanted to get it done as soon as possible so she could get back to selling her cupcakes.

"Things are going great. People love my cupcakes," Mia said happily. She had spent all the previous evening baking cupcakes to sell today.

"That's great. Now you have nothing but happy customers." Sophie was wearing new shoes which were sparkling in the sunlight.

"Well, mostly. I'm still running out of cupcakes. But I can't think of a way to make more cupcakes," Mia replied. It was a problem that she had been thinking about for the last few days. A problem she still needed to figure out.

"You will think of something," Sophie smiled. She was skipping, kicking he legs high, admiring her new shoes.

"Always do," Mia said, determined. "Want to come in and do the math homework together?"

"Yes. Let's get it done. I don't want to annoy Mr Frost. Did you see the way he shouted at Dan today?"

"I would be so embarrassed if he shouted at me like that. But Dan really shouldn't be filming himself making videos in class."

The front window of the house hung open as the girls arrived. The sounds of laughing and music could be heard from the end of the driveway. "Sounds like Tom's basketball team."

"Are they always so loud," Sophie asked.

"Always," Mia answered. "Come on, we can get some snacks in the kitchen and go to my room."

The kitchen was packed full of Tom's friends. They were lunging on chairs, dancing to music, laughing and joking.

Mia's heart froze at the sight of them. Each of them had a mouthful of cupcakes, Mia's cupcakes. Everywhere she looked, there were half-eaten cupcakes. Crumbs littered the floor, falling from munching mouths. Tom was in the middle of the chaos, a cupcake in each hand.

Mia wanted to scream, to shout, to throw something at Tom. But she couldn't move, couldn't speak. She stood frozen in the doorway, mouth hanging open.

"Mia." Sophie's hand was on her shoulder. "Are you ok?"

"I.. I.." Mia mumbled. She couldn't find the words. Her product was destroyed. She would have to send her customers away. She could see their sad, disappointed faces twisting in her mind. She would need to buy more supplies, which would take away all her profits. Not to mention the time it would take to bake it all again. This was a disaster.

"What's up, pipsqueak?" Tom sauntered over to Mia, cupcakes crumbling in his hands as he walked. "Cupcakes are great. Everyone loves them."

Mia almost punched him then. In fact, she was pretty sure Sophie almost punched him too. "How could you?" Mia crocked, voice breaking, but she wouldn't let herself cry in front of Tom.

"What? Cupcakes are meant to be eaten, are they not?" Tom swept his hands around the room. "And look how everyone is enjoying them."

All of Tom's friends cheered at that, raising their cupcakes, Mia's cupcakes in the air.

Mia spun around and stormed out of the room.

"You're a mean big brother," Sophie told Tom before stomping hard on Tom's foot.

"AHH, that hurt," Tom yelped.

"It was supposed to," Sophie snapped back.

"Come on, why are you both upset? It's not a big deal," Tom called after the girls as they hurried up the stairs.

Chapter 16

Mia was curled up on her bed. It was still light out, but Mia had the blanket over her head. Her pillow was wet with tears. Sophie had left a while ago; Mia didn't feel up to talking about things. She was so mad and sad. She didn't know what to do next.

"Mia!" Mum's voice was muffled with her head under blankets. Mia closed her eyes and tried to ignore the world.

"Mia!" Mum called again, sounding more annoyed the second time.

"Mia, answer your mum!" Dad chipped in before Mia could even think about answering.

"What?" Mia shouted back, maybe a little too angrily. Mia stomped to the door, hair messy, tears still on her cheeks.

"You have customers," Mum shouted up the stairs.

OH NO! Mia thought. She had promised loads of people more cupcakes would be available today. What was she going to tell them now? She wanted to run, hide, or cower under her blanket and never come out.

"Mia," Mum called again. "There are loads of people here. Come now."

Shoulders slumped, Mia trudged down the stairs, each step agonisingly slow.

"Mia!" Mum shouted again. "Oh, there you are," Mum spotted Mia on the stairs.

"You have got loads of people waiting outside. Better hurry up."

Mia felt like she was going to vomit. Mia was met with a sea of smiling faces. Most of the people she recognised, but there were a few new faces. Seeing them, Mia felt even more like she was going to vomit.

"Cupcakes! Woo!" someone shouted from the back. Everyone cheered in response.

"Um," Mia mumbled.

"Can I get four?" the first customer asked. She was a tall woman with a hint of white in her hair and a missing tooth on one side.

"Um, I, um," Mia stumbled. All these people were looking at her; it broke her heart to let them down. She had worked so hard to build her customer base, and she was about to destroy their trust. "I'm sorry, I don't have any cupcakes today."

"What?"

"Are you joking?"

"This can't be serious!"

"We have been queuing for nothing!"

Mia was hit by a wave of disgruntled voices. "I'm sorry. I will have more ready first thing tomorrow."

"I'll not be back!" Mia heard someone say.

"Me either. She told us there would be cupcakes today. I, for one, won't trust her again."

The crowd started to disperse, slowly at first, then all at once. Finally, Mia was left standing all alone on her front porch.

Chapter 17

Hand on the railing, Mia made her way back up to her bedroom. She would get back under her blankets. Hide from the world and not think about baking again. It had been good while it lasted, Mia thought.

She made her way back to her cave one step at a time. About halfway up, she froze. Hand gripping the railing, Mia thought about everything she had accomplished so far. She thought about how much fun she had learning to bake, finding customers, and making people happy. Was she really going to give all that up?

"Mia, are you ok?" Mum asked from the bottom of the stairs. "Standing in the middle of the stairs is a bit weird." Mum's lycra was yellow today, and she was carrying a hula hoop for some reason.

"Yeah, I'm ok," Mia said. "Mum."

"Yes, dear."

"Preheat the oven. It's time to bake."

Mia wasn't going to be beaten, not by Tom, not by anyone.

She baked all night, one batch after another. By the following morning, Mia was bleary-eyed, standing in her kitchen. Her eyes were red and stinging with tiredness.

Mia sat on the floor, surrounded by delicious little cupcake towers. Stacked around her were dozens and dozens of freshly made cupcakes. Mia was exhausted, but she wasn't done.

The sun was barely up when Mia pushed a little trolley stacked with boxes of her cupcakes down the driveway.

The trolley was old and rickety; one wheel stuck a little and pulled the trolley to the left. Mia had to fight to keep it going straight.

She hauled her trolley up Mr Khans, her next-door neighbour's drive. She was huffing and puffing by the time she made it to the front door.

The door was heavy oak; it made a solid thud when Mia struck the knocker.

"Mia, what are you doing here this early?" Mr Khan wore a dressing gown, and his thick black hair was sticking up like he had just gotten out of bed.

"Sorry to wake you so early, Mr Khan," Mia said. "I know a lot of the neighbours were very disappointed that I had no cupcakes available yesterday."

"Oh yes, my wife was very disappointed. And I must say I was looking forward to some myself." Mr Khan's noticed Mia's trolley full of cupcakes for the first time and licked his lips.

"Well then, I have great news. To apologise for letting you and your wife down, I wanted to come by and give you a couple free cupcakes to make up for it." Mia handed over a box of cupcakes.

"Thank you. This is so nice, and my wife will be delighted."

"I'm glad you're happy. I hope you and your wife will be customers again soon," Mia said, smiling.

"Absolutely," Mr Khan said, already scoffing down half a cupcake.

"Great, see you soon," Mia laughed as Mr Khans' nose was covered in thick blue icing.

Mia could hear Mr Khan calling to his wife as he dragged the trolley back down the drive.

She looked down the street, rows of houses on either side. Mia could hear the sounds of morning all around her: birds chirping, dogs being let out for a walk, and kids being woken up.

Mia had a lot of work to do, but she wouldn't stop before she delivered free cupcakes to all of her neighbours.

One wheel of her trolley gave up and ran away just as Mia finished her deliveries. Mia didn't have the energy to chase it; she just watched as it disappeared down the street.

Her arms were burning from dragging the wreckage of her trolley home. She collapsed on the porch; the trolley tipped up behind her. She was exhausted; she could sleep right there under the sun, with those summer flies buzzing at her head.

Mia crawled into the house. Her arms were sore, her legs were sore, and her trolley was broken, but Mia was delighted. All the neighbours loved their free cupcakes; Mia thought she had repaired a lot of the damage that had been done to her reputation yesterday.

"Mia! Why are you on the floor?" Mum stood over her in a tracksuit, swigging a green tea.

Mia continued to crawl. "Mum, preheat the oven."

Mia felt a bit wobbly as she lifted a hand to wave Mum into the kitchen. "Time to bake."

"No," Mum said firmly.

"But," Mia started, "I have to."

"Mia, you can't work yourself into the ground. If you want to be successful, you need to look after yourself first," Mum looked concerned. "You can't provide a service for others if you can't keep your eyes open."

"But," Mia protested, but her eyes kept closing, which didn't help her argument.

"Your mum is right." Dad appeared out of the living room, hiding a chocolate wrapper in his pocket before Mum could see.

Before Mia could say anymore, Dad scooped her up in his arms. "Time for bed," Dad said.

"Ok," Mia said, giving up; maybe she could sleep just a little. "But then, it'll be time to bake." Mia was asleep before Dad dropped her in bed.

Chapter 18

Business was back and booming. The days flew by, and Mia was a whirlwind, bake, sell, bake more, sell more. It was crazy. It was exhausting. It was amazing.

Money was rolling in now. Cupcakes were selling as fast as she could make them.

The cupcakes lined up on the counter, neat little smiley faces iced on top. Mia's hair was in a tight bun, her tongue sticking out as she focused on perfecting the icing on her latest batch. Mia was completely focused.

"Mia!" Tom's voice sounded right behind her. Mia jumped, turning her perfect smiley face icing upside down.

"Tom, look what you made me do." Mia tried to fix it but made it much worse.

"Are they supposed to look like goblins?" Tom asked, peeking over Mia's shoulder.

"No, they are smiley faces," Mia retorted, not looking at Tom. Mia was still furious with Tom for taking her money and eating her cupcakes.

"Have you ever seen a smiley face?"

"Are you just here to make fun of me, or are you planning on destroying more of my cupcakes." Mia could feel her anger bubbling again; her skin felt hot.

"No, I'm here to say sorry."

"What?" Mia was shocked. Anger flooded out of her, replaced with confusion. Tom never apologised, not ever.

"I'm sorry."

"Are you joking?" Tom was always playing jokes on Mia.

"No, I'm really sorry. I shouldn't have ruined your cupcakes. That was mean." Mia looked at Tom then, his head was down, and he was pulling at his hair. He seemed really sad.

"Then why'd you do it?" Mia didn't want to let Tom off the hook and wasn't sure she trusted him. The memory of all her ruined cupcakes was still fresh and raw.

"Honestly, I was jealous."

"You were jealous of me?" Mia was shocked. Tom had always been the cool one. Tom had loads of friends, was captain of the basketball team, and everyone liked him.

"I guess I was. Everyone loves your cupcakes; the whole street was talking about them. I guess I got jealous and lashed out. I'm sorry, I shouldn't have done that." Tom was still looking at the floor. He looked as awkward as Mia felt.

"It's ok, I guess," Mia said. She didn't know what to make of Tom's apology, but she knew she didn't feel angry anymore.

"I wanted to ask something else," Tom asked.

Here it comes; Mia thought I knew he wasn't being serious; he just wanted to make a joke out of me.

"Can I help?" Tom asked

"Help? With what?" Mia was even more confused.

"With selling your cupcakes. You said before you need some help," Tom continued. "I thought I could do that."

Mia was sure she was misunderstanding something. Tom wanted to help her; she was so confused. "You want to help? That means you would need to do what I say?" Mia said.

"I know," Tom replied. "But I would get paid?"

"Of course," Mia said, trying to sound as professional as possible. Tom nodded at that; he looked excited and relieved. "Be down here first thing in the morning to get started."

"Absolutely. See you in the morning." Tom rushed off before Mia could change her mind.

Just like that, Mia had her first employee.

Chapter 19

It was just as hot and just as busy once Mia opened her shop the following day. People were queuing up at the edge of the garden, but with Tom there to help, things went much smoother.

Tom was excellent with the customers. Tom had always been good with people; he was funny and easy to talk to. He must have told his friends; half the basketball team were in the queue by the end of the morning.

As soon as Mia realised they were running low on cupcakes, she ran back inside and started another batch. With Tom handling the sales out front Mia kept the cupcakes coming. Mia definitely would not run out of cupcakes again.

Mia was setting out a new batch of lemon cupcakes when a big shadow fell over her. It was like a giant had reached up and blotted out the sun. Mia looked up to see Mr Baxter looming over the table.

"Mr Baxter. How can I help you?" Mia asked. Mia put on her biggest smile. Mr Baxter was on her turf now, and she wouldn't let him intimidate her.

"Came to see what all the fuss was about," Mr Baxter said with his deep voice. A few people behind him in the queue took a step back. Seemed like Mr Baxter scared more people than just Mia.

"And?" Mia asked.

"I'm impressed. I didn't think you would have it in you. Let me have 5 to try; I'm interested." He smiled, showing all his teeth, it reminded Mia of a lion about to pounce, but she thought he meant well.

Mia couldn't believe what she was hearing or seeing. Mia happily packaged up 5 cupcakes for the tall man.

"Would you like some lemonade as well?" Mia asked.

"Don't push your luck." Mr Baxter stalked away down the street.

Mia couldn't help but laugh. She was delighted she was proving everyone wrong. First, her brother and now Mr Baxter.

Chapter 20

Mia was buzzing. Another hard day's work, but she was finally starting to feel like her business was becoming a success. She couldn't stop thinking about the possibilities to make it even better.

One big problem kept spinning in her head, a problem that she didn't think she could fix - the weather. In fact, she was pretty sure she couldn't do anything to control the weather; that would have been pretty cool though.

There were only a few weeks left of summer. The autumn would bring a lot of things, crinkly brown leaves, squirrels scuttling about collecting nuts, and Dad would start collecting wood for winter fires. But more importantly, the new season would bring winds and rain. Mia was sure people wouldn't be queuing on the edge of her garden in a storm. She could imagine Mr Winters standing in his thick purple cardigan, soaked through with rain and shivering in the cold. No, Mia thought, people definitely won't want to stand in the cold. Besides, her cupcakes would get soaked, and damp cupcakes did not sound one bit appetising.

Mia needed to solve this problem quick; otherwise, her cupcake business would be washed down the gutter in a few weeks.

Laying on her bed at night, she tried to come up with a solution. Dad had painted stars on the ceiling of her bedroom a year ago; they glowed a soft green in the dark. Mia thought of how far she had come over the last few months. She never would have believed this a year ago. She thought about all her happy customers. Then another idea hit her. Mia smiled as she went to sleep. She had more work to do in the morning.

Chapter 21

Bright and early the next morning, the bell rang as Mia opened the door of Mr Baxter's shop. Mr Baxter was towering over the counter as usual.

The shop looked like it always did, which is to say, it was a mess. Someone had stacked a tower of eggs on top of some toilet roll; the whole thing wobbled slightly whenever someone walked past. Mia would be shocked if someone didn't leave the store that day covered in eggs.

"Mia, how can I help you?" Mr Baxter's voice boomed through the shop. He seemed much friendlier than ever before.

"How were the cupcakes?" Mia started.

"Delicious, I have to hand it to you, kid; they really were delicious," Mr Baxter said. "You have me beat there. Can't compete with you and those cupcakes. I have never been much of a baker myself."

"That's what I want to talk to you about," Mia said cautiously.

"You want me to compete with you?" Mr. Baxter said, confused.

"No, no," Mia said, "I was thinking more of a partnership."

"I'm listening," said Mr Baxter intrigued. He rested his hands on the counter and leaned closer to Mia like they were sharing a secret. They were, in fact, doing that, Mia supposed.

"Well, I was thinking that I could sell you large batches of cupcakes at a discounted rate, and then you could sell them on to your customers, and that way, we could both make a profit."

Mr Baxter started rubbing his chin. "Interesting. I need to be getting a good rate."

"Of course, We can definitely work out a reasonable price." Mia could tell Mr Baxter was very interested.

"I'd say about fifty per cent discount would be reasonable," Mr Baxter said.

Mia had expected Mr Baxter to be a tough negotiator and thought he would try something like this. Fifty per cent discount was far too much. Fortunately, Mia was prepared and would not be caught off guard. If she agreed to a fifty per cent discount, Mr

Baxter would make a fortune, but Mia would make almost nothing.

"Oh no, Mr Baxter, that just wouldn't do. I was thinking more of a ten per cent discount," Mia replied. Mr Baxter was staring at her intently now. Mia didn't look away.

"Mia, I know you are new to the business world, so I will try not to be offended by your offer. I think my offer of fifty per cent is more than reasonable. You must understand this is how business works. Think of how many more cupcakes you will sell from a store than your garden." Mr Baxter smiled his toothy smile again, reminding Mia of a hyena about to eat its dinner. "In fact, as a sign of good faith, I will be generous and accept your deal at a forty-five per cent discount. Final offer."

Mr Baxter stuck his hand out to shake on the deal; his hand reminded Mia of a bear's paw.

"Sorry to hear that, Mr Baxter, but if that's your final offer. I can't accept," Mia turned away, "I have had a lot of interest in my cupcakes. I gave you the first offer, given we are such good friends, but I'll just have to check with Miss Turner's shop or the supermarket to see if they are interested."

Mia was halfway out of the store when Mr Baxter called her back. "Mia, don't be so hasty; we are still discussing. No need to be going anywhere near that old crow Miss Turner."

Miss Turner was Mr Baxter's biggest rival; their shops were always competing with each other on prices and customers. Mia, of course, knew this, and that's why she had mentioned Miss Turner in the first place.

"I could probably do a twenty per cent discount," Mr Baxter said, a little bead of sweat forming on his forehead and trickling down his cheek.

Twenty per cent was a big difference from his forty-five per cent final offer two minutes ago. Mia almost leapt at the offer, almost, but she thought she could push it a little bit further.

"How about we meet halfway at a fifteen per cent discount?" Mia asked

She could see the cogs running in Mr Baxter's brain. She knew he was thinking about Miss Turner's store overflowing with customers buying Mia's cupcakes.

"Alright, I am happy to try it. You've got a deal," he said, reaching down his massive hand to shake Mia's little one. His handshake almost lifted Mia off her feet.

"Fantastic!" Mia said, delighted.

Mia left the shop ecstatic. Now she didn't have to worry about the weather; she could sell them from Mr Baxter's shop instead. Plus, Mr Baxter's store had loads of customers, so she would have loads more potential customers.

Chapter 22

For the next few weeks, Mia delivered cupcakes daily to Mr Baxter's shop. Mr Baxter was delighted they were great sellers, and Mr Baxter was buying more and more cupcakes from Mia every day.

Mia switched Tom from selling to helping with the baking. Tom wasn't a great baker to start, but he worked hard, followed instructions well, and got better and better.

Mia was glad, too, as she was making more and more cupcakes with Tom's help. She even had more time to try more recipes.

Mum spent a whole week complaining that Mia had no healthy cupcake options. Mum had suggested a kale cupcake, and Dad had vomited at the thought.

Mia did think a healthier option was a good business opportunity. Mia thought many health-conscious people, like her Mum, would be interested in a healthy choice. It took a lot of work to get a working recipe. Finally, Mia managed a cupcake with raisins, dates and half as much sugar. Mum loved it, and Dad agreed that it tasted great. It turned out to be one of Mia's best sellers.

Chapter 23

A few days later, the weather had definitely changed. The ground was wet, and little puddles collected on the sides of the road. Chilly winds blew clusters of crunchy brown leaves across the pavement.

Mia was warped in a thick jumper and woolly socks. She stood outside the bike store with a handful of money. Bikes in myriad colours and sizes shone on display through the window. Smiling and giggling, Mia dragged her Mum inside.

Minutes later, Mia rode out of the store on a shiny new red bike. Mia started to ride in circles around her Mum.

Mia tested the new bell and couldn't help but laugh with joy at the ringing sound. Mia thought back to that day in the park seeing those kids on their new bikes racing through the crowds. Mia had thought about that moment dozens of times since. She had done so much work since then, from her lemonade stand to cupcakes to working with Mr Baxter. It had been hard work, really hard at times, but it has also been so much fun. Mia had learned so much and made new friends with Mr Baxter and Tom. Now she was on her new bike spinning around the car park in front of the bike store

Mia's Mum asked, "So, was it worth it?"

"Absolutely!!" Mia replied immediately.

"At least now you can take a break from selling cupcakes," her Mum said.

"Break? No way I'm having too much fun. Everybody is going to be buying my cupcakes. I've got even bigger plans for the future."

With that, Mia rode off down the street laughing while her Mum chased after her. Mia knew she was just getting started.

THE END

Printed in Great Britain
by Amazon